Teaching Children About Food

A Teaching and Activities Guide

Christine Berman, MPH, RD
and
Jacki Fromer

Bull Publishing Company
Palo Alto, California

Copyright © 1991 Bull Publishing Company

Bull Publishing Company
P.O. Box 208
Palo Alto, California 94302-0208
(415) 322-2855

ISBN 0-923521-15-1

Distributed in the U.S. by:
Publishers Group West
4065 Hollis Street
Emeryville, CA 94608

Library of Congress
Cataloging-in-Publication Data
Berman, Christine.
      Teaching Children about food / by Christine Berman and
Jacki Fromer.
            p.   cm.
      Includes bibliographical references and index.
      ISBN 0-923521-15-1
            1. Nutrition—Study and teaching (Elementary)
            2. Cookery—Study and teaching (Elementary)
      I. Fromer, Jacki.   II. Title.
      TX364B47   1991
      372.3'7044—dc20   91-4245
                                                           CIP

Cover Design: Robb Pawlak
Cover Photographer: Zeva Longley
Interior Design: Maura McAndrew
Production Manager: Helen O'Donnell
Compositor: The Cowans
Display and Text Face: Palatino
Printer: Bookcrafters, Inc.

First printing: August 1991

Contents

Acknowledgements

Special thanks to Carol Larson for generosity of time and computer expertise in spite of an incredibly busy schedule, Reed Fromer and Peter White for guidance in editing and organizing, and David Fromer for artistry, and those invaluable, enthusiastic pep talks.

And with loving appreciation—

To our family members for their assistance, encouragement, confidence, suggestions, patience and love—David, Reed and Rachel Fromer, Mitch Berman, Wynter and Mai Grant, Carol, Brad, Matthew and Sierra Larson, Ann Spake and Jon Fromer.

To our dear friends and associates for their ideas, critiques, generosity, enthusiasm, moral support, friendship and recipes — Barbara Abrams, DRPH, RD; Rita Abrams; Charlotte Albert; Pat Ayotte; Katy Baer, MPH, RD; Nina Baker; Judy Bartlett; Linda Bartshire; Elaine Belle; Georgia Berry; Ruth Bramell; Canal Child Care Center; Marek Cepietz; Doris Disbrow, DRPH, RD; Doris Fredericks, MED, RD; Elazar Freidman; Diana Goodrow; Robin Goodrow and Vanilla; Gail Hartman; Geri Henchy, MPH, RD; Bev Hoffman; Paula James; Sally Jones; Steven Kipperman; DeLona Kurtz; the staff of Marin Head Start; Elizabeth McGrady; Eileen Nelson; Katie O'Neill, MPH, RD; Lloyd Partch; Bayla Penman; Karen Jeffrey Pertschuk, MPH, RD; Johanne Quinlan; Helen Rossini; Zak Sabry, PHD; Ellyn Satter, RD, ACSW; Jackie Shonerd; Steve Susskind; The Earth Store; Barbara Taylor; Steve Thompson; Kate Warin; Rona Weintraub; Peter White; Barbara Zeavin; Jill Zwicky, and the Marin Child Care Council staff members: Emilie Albertoli, Lynne Arceneaux, Terry DeMartini, Teresa Leibert, Mary Moore, Susan Sanders, and Hilda Castillo Wilson.

To the wonderful people at Bull Publishing for the opportunity to bring our project to fruition.

In loving memory and admiration of Florence Raskin, Katherine Fromer and Necia "Ida" Fromer.

And for the continuing inspiration we receive from child care providers and teachers who are dedicated to the well-being of children.

Introduction

Because eating is such a basic, necessary human function, comparable to sleeping or breathing, it's easy to overlook the fact that children have a lot to learn about food. Ideally, they will grow up to eat healthfully, enjoy meals, and be socially responsible in their food-related habits.

Children's education in this area doesn't ordinarily come in the form of prepared "lessons," but rather takes place through spontaneous suggestions or instructions ("Don't put so much sugar on your cereal . . . ," etc.), and observation (what they see others doing). Children frequently see adults eat meals too rich in fat and sugar, or skip meals because they're "dieting." They may also see adults throw bottles and cans into the garbage rather than in the recycling bin.

Therefore, it is important for the adults who are caring for children to set appropriate examples. With people facing so many health problems related to eating habits, and our environment suffering from our poor consumption habits, it is crucial to start "food education" at an early age with good role models.

It has been our experience that every child care setting has its own needs related to food and mealtime. Some children arrive at a preschool scarcely able to manage a fork, while others can tell you in excruciating detail why they don't eat fatty foods. *Teaching Children About Food* is not a custom-made nutrition curriculum with prescribed activities on a monthly schedule, but rather an overview of important subject areas and useful methods of "food awareness."

We have tried to provide a framework by which you can tailor your very own "food education program." The basic concepts that children need to learn about food are the same everywhere; how you teach them will be up to you, although we do include some specific suggestions which may be useful.

This book is intended to be used with its companion volume, *Meals Without Squeals*, a child care feeding guide and cookbook. The reason we emphasize this is not because we want to sell another book, but because the foods you serve and the way you approach mealtimes are very powerful (and often overlooked) vehicles of nutrition education. It is important to make them consistent with what you are teaching in other areas of food education. We think that you'll find the recipes and menu plans, hints for mealtime management, and coverage of child nutrition issues in *Meals Without Squeals* very useful as the foundation for your food education program.

CHAPTER ONE

A Basic Scheme for Nutrition Education

Planning Nutrition Education for Children

Children start learning about food and nutrition when they're tiny babies. The way their caregivers handle feeding them by breast or by bottle, and then later the meals they share with family members and other people, the television shows and commercials they see, and the books they read, all contribute to the feelings and ideas that children will come to associate with eating in general, and foods in particular. Unfortunately, not all of these feelings and ideas are positive or health-promoting.

When we plan nutrition education for children, we are attempting to make learning experiences in the realm of food and nutrition intentional, rather than accidental. And what do we expect will be the end result of this effort? Well, hopefully these youngsters will grow up to be adults who eat healthfully, feel good about eating, are tolerant of other people's eating choices, and act as responsible consumers.

Are you with us so far? Good. Now let's review what children must learn (and believe) in order for this to happen:

- ❑ When they are hungry, their needs will be met.
- ❑ Their own food preferences will be respected.
- ❑ Eating is an enjoyable activity.

- There are ways to deal with uncomfortable feelings, besides eating.
- People in different cultures, and families within those cultures, have different ways of eating and different ways of celebrating special occasions with food.
- Our food choices influence our well-being.
- Food is made available through the efforts of many members of the community.
- In order to eat, we use up resources, and we create waste that needs to be dealt with responsibly.

There are numerous themes you can develop in order to support these basic concepts. Some are simple enough for a toddler to grasp, others are more complicated and are best used with older children. For example, a preschooler can learn that we need food in order to live and grow; a sixth grader can learn the role of protein or calcium in maintaining our bodies' functions.

Here are enough themes to last you for years! Remember, the simpler concepts serve as a foundation for learning the more complicated ones:[1]

Simpler

- I need to wash my hands before handling food or eating.
- I must behave in an acceptable fashion at the meal table.
- There are lots of different foods I can eat.
- I can name foods of different sizes, shapes, colors, and preparation methods.
- I can enjoy and identify foods using all of my senses.
- I need to eat a variety of good foods in order to grow and stay healthy.
- I can identify foods that come from animals.
- I can identify foods that come from plants.
- I know how the plants that we eat grow.

- Many people work to give me the food I eat . . . farmers, food processors, truck drivers, grocers, bakers, parents, caregivers . . .

- People in different cultures eat different foods, and families within those cultures eat different foods and use certain foods to celebrate special occasions.

- Television advertising will try to get me to buy foods that aren't always good for me.

- Food has to be stored and handled carefully or it can make me sick when I eat it.

- I should avoid wasting food.

- When I eat, I make waste that I should dispose of in a way that is best for the earth.

- I can describe the relationship between what I eat and the health of my teeth.

- I can make myself healthful snacks and help grownups prepare meals.

- I can identify practices that ensure my safety while cooking.

- I need to balance my food intake with work and play activities.

More Difficult

- ❏ I can classify foods by food group.

- ❏ I can name one major nutrient provided by each of the food groups.

- ❏ I can plan a nutritionally adequate meal.

- ❏ I can name at least one function for each of the six major nutrient groups.

- ❏ I can describe the basic process of digestion.

- ❏ I can name foods that are significant sources of protein, starches, sugar, fat, sodium, and fiber.

- ❏ I can name several health professionals that give advice regarding the relationship between food and health.

- ❏ I can recognize the main ingredients in certain products by reading their food labels.

- ❏ I can use unit pricing to decide what's the best buy when purchasing foods.

How Do Children Learn About Nutrition?

There are lots of ways, actually. And you need to consider all of them when you're planning a program of nutrition education:

Your menus . . . which are a statement about what you feel are appropriate foods to eat, and which can either serve to broaden children's awareness about foods or can limit it.

Modeling adult behavior . . . when children see you enjoying a variety of good foods, being willing to try new foods, being mannerly at the table, respecting the food choices of other people, and making an effort to recycle food containers, it makes an impression on them. When they see you wasting food, drinking soda pop all day long, or depriving yourself of food while dieting, it also makes an impression on them. That's why it is important that adults who are working with children be nutritionally aware and mindful of their actions.

Nutrition concepts in the environment . . . picture books, puzzles, play foods or empty food packages in the playhouse, pictures on the wall, games, television shows and videos, and stickers used as rewards or decorations, all should be looked at with a critical eye. What messages are they imparting about the value of certain foods or eating practices?

Formal learning activities and field trips . . . their frequency and complexity must depend on the age of the child. Young children won't benefit from a lecture, but they can be set up with opportunities to explore foods by manipulating them, learn songs about handwashing, and visit farms or grow their own food in gardens or sprouting projects. Older children can learn from games, science experiments, and other activities.

Cooking activities . . . allow children to feel, smell, and taste new foods, to feel good about themselves as they contribute to meals eaten by others, and to become more self-sufficient in their eating.

Reinforcement at home . . . ensures consistent messages. Parents and caregivers or teachers should be in communication with each other about the values and concepts they are trying to impart to the children. Opportunities can be given to parents to participate in the nutrition programs at their childrens' schools and child care sites (page 8).

Now, it isn't our intention to lay out an entire nutrition curriculum for you. But we would like to encourage you to look at your nutrition education program systematically, and give you some of our ideas for activities, along with some resources for others.

We have found it helps to be able to organize your thoughts on paper. The *Food Education Planner* on page 9 is an example using the theme "There are lots of different foods I can eat" we discuss below. We have included a blank form on page 10 for you to photocopy and use when planning your program.

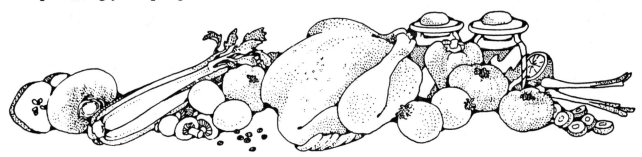

First let's walk through the different ways one of the themes discussed earlier could be taught. Suppose, for example, we want four-year-olds to get the idea that "there are lots of different foods that I can eat."

Theme:	There Are Lots of Different Foods I Can Eat
The menu:	A variety of tasty and attractive foods are served, some familiar to the children and some new to them.
Modeling:	The children see adults enjoying a variety of foods and being willing to taste new ones.
Concepts in environment:	Books and posters portray a vast assortment of foods, some familiar and some more unusual. Some books that talk about eating a variety of foods are:

> *Bread and Jam for Frances* (R. Hoban, Harper & Row, Publisher, New York, 1964).
>
> *Gregory the Terrible Eater* (M. Sharmat, Scholastic Book Service, New York, 1980).
>
> *Green Eggs and Ham* (Dr. Seuss, Random House, New York, 1960).

Activities and trips:	Take a field trip to an ethnic grocery store, a farmers' market, or the produce department of a local supermarket. Help the children pick out some food items they've never tasted, then go back home or to the classroom and have a tasting party.
	Make a flannelboard story out of *Green Eggs and Ham*. (For added fun, the next day let the children tell you the story).
	Sing a song together about trying new foods (see page 59).
Cooking:	Make "Green Eggs and Ham" together.
	Prepare some of the foods from the above field trip with the children.

❏ ❏ ❏

"Green" Eggs and Ham

8 eggs	*oil*
1/2 cup minced fresh parsley (chives are also nice, but optional)	*4 oz. cooked turkey ham or Canadian bacon*
1/2 cup milk	*salt and pepper to taste*

1. Beat eggs, parsley, and milk together.
2. Scramble egg mixture in a heavy or nonstick pan in a small amount of oil.
3. Serve with small amounts of turkey ham or Canadian bacon on the side.

Serves 8 preschool or school-age children
1 meat

❏ ❏ ❏

At home:	Send recipes home to parents, using new foods introduced in school or child care.

Making the Most of Your Position as a Role Model

Children are constantly learning from what adults do and say. By "labeling" our actions, and explaining the "why's" when we make choices, we are making the most of our opportunity to help children learn. Remember to talk with children (without "lecturing") about what you are doing and why you are doing it. Also consider how your conversations with other adults may influence children who might be listening.

Here are some examples:

- ❏ "Let's clear our food garbage into this empty carton and add it to the compost. Instead of filling up the garbage dumps, we'll be making new soil."

- ❏ "I'll rinse this jar and add it to the recycling bin. Glass can be reused over and over again."

- ❏ "Let's bring our canvas bag to the grocery store. That way we don't need to use either paper or plastic bags."

- ❏ "While we're brushing our teeth, let's turn off the faucet so we won't be wasting water."

- ❏ "I was going to buy this cereal, but I just read the label and saw how much salt and sugar it had. I'll buy this other kind instead."

- ❏ "Let's buy the eggs in the cardboard carton instead of in the plastic foam one. That way we can recycle and we won't be adding to pollution."

Acknowledge efforts that the children make to follow your examples. Let them know that you notice when they learn something new.

SAMPLE

Food Education Planner

Central idea __There are lots of different foods to eat__

Menu	Role Modeling
Try new vegetables (with dip): jicama, asparagus, snow peas. Try vietnamese soup recipe from Tran's mom.	Talk about how much fun it is to explore new foods, while we're eating lunch.

Environment	Activities
Put Green Eggs and Ham in book area (also read during circle time). Put up poster of exotic produce.	Field trip to Asian Food Mart for materials for Nori-Maki rolls.

Cooking Projects	Parents/"Homework"
"Green Eggs and Ham" Nori-Maki rolls	Send recipes home for Nori-Maki rolls and Tran's mom's soup, along with write-up of tips for introducing new foods.

Food Education Planner

Central idea _____

Menu	Role Modeling

Environment	Activities

Cooking Projects	Parents/"Homework"

CHAPTER TWO

The Social Aspects
of Food

Planting Seeds for Healthy Children and a Healthy Planet

Food preparation and mealtimes offer opportunities to model and teach healthy and responsible behavior towards self, others and our world. The experiences we provide help to plant the seeds of curiosity, interest, understanding and caring in children. Some of the concepts we can begin to teach in relation to mealtime include:

- ❑ How food is grown, produced, transported, marketed, cooked, etc.

- ❑ How to be smart, thoughtful shoppers—economically, environmentally, and healthwise.

- ❑ How to responsibly dispose of leftover food and food packaging.

- ❑ What responsibilities we have toward others—from appropriate behavior when eating together to awareness of global issues such as world hunger, environmental protection, etc.

- ❑ Respect and appreciation for the diversity of lifestyles among people.

Knowing how much our day-to-day actions influence the development of children in our care can be a strong motivating factor in helping us to keep striving toward more healthy and environmentally sound habits. By functioning in a way that reflects concern and caring for our own well-being and that of others we are taking the first step toward helping the children we care for begin to grow into healthy and responsible adults.

Food and the Development of Social Awareness

The need for food is, of course, one of the primary things that all human beings have in common. Because of this, mealtime can serve as the first setting for developing a child's social awareness.

This development takes place in many stages and in many "arenas." In a preschool setting this awareness is very direct and personal. For example, children begin to gain a sense of manners and consideration for others (such as, passing food at the table, not taking "seconds" until everyone has had "firsts," the concept of sharing) which they can, hopefully, start to apply to other non-mealtime areas of interaction. They are also learning about the ways in which they are the same as, as well as different from each other, through seeing and hearing about each other's families.

More appropriate at a later age, 5 years and up, when a child begins to see the world as involving more than just his direct experience, is the fostering of an awareness of a larger scope of social concerns and cultural traits. Children are learning that there is a whole world of people, and that there is an immense diversity of customs, beliefs, ways of life—and an equally immense, and shocking, diversity of economic conditions and abilities to meet nutritional needs.

Teaching Children About Hunger

How and when do children become aware that for many people hunger means far more than just having to wait an half hour until snack time? What role can adults take in helping children (who have not experienced it first-hand) understand and deal with this awareness?

Again, it is most appropriate to introduce these concepts to children of five years and up because:

1. They may be hearing or seeing things that make them curious—What is Ethiopia? Why was that man back there sleeping on the street?

2. They are getting old enough to learn about some harsh realities without becoming overly frightened or seeing themselves as being in danger.

3. They are capable of taking some actions (participation in food drives, etc.) which have results that they can see and/or understand; this helps to instill a sense of empowerment— "I can help solve the problem!"

The purpose of teaching children about hunger is not to get them to eat their broccoli. Telling them to "finish your vegetables, there are children starving in India" to an adult means "you should appreciate the fact that *you* have food." But a child might easily miss the connection, and feel confused: What does *my* broccoli have to do with someone I don't even know?

Ideally, as we teach children about hunger and other social problems and injustices, we are helping them grow into adults who will care about society and the world, and who will feel capable and motivated to keep improving it. We need to teach them in a way that neither minimizes nor exaggerates the problem of hunger. How can we accomplish this?

The book, *Discover the World: Empowering Children to Value Themselves, Others and the Earth*, edited by Susan Hopkins and Jeffry Winters, offers many suggestions and "activity charts" designed to help adults teach children about social concerns. We have included their activity chart related to the issue of hunger on page 16. The activities are appropriate for use with preschool and early elementary school-age children.

Older elementary school children and junior high and high school age children are capable of learning, understanding and doing much more in relation to hunger.

They should never be made to feel guilty or responsible for the plight of others, but can learn ways in which they can contribute to improving things. The *Food First Curriculum* by Laurie Rubin, a publication from the Institute for Food and Development Policy in San Francisco, CA, is an excellent resource. It is described as "an integrated curriculum to help Grade 6 students learn the paths of the food they eat, the roots of hunger here and abroad, and how they can act locally on a global problem; with modifications for Grades 4–5 and 7–8." It is filled with educational activities, interesting and challenging for adults as well as for children, which address topics such as:

- ❏ *Why Do People Around the World Do Things in So Many Different Ways?*
- ❏ *Where Does Our Food Come From?*
- ❏ *Why Are People Hungry?*
- ❏ *What Can We Do?*

To order a copy of the book, call or write: Institute for Food and Development Policy, 1885 Mission Street, San Francisco, CA 94103 (415) 864-8555.

Learning About Hunger: Activity Chart

Concept ⟶	Good nutrition involves eating a balanced diet of various foods	We can grow food.	Not everyone has as much food as they would like.	Sharing means giving of ourselves to help others.	We can share food with our neighbors.
Art Experience ⟶	Make a collage with food pictures representing the food groups.	Paint pictures of gardens or farms.		Make a picture book about sharing.	
Science Experience ⟶	Make a food group mural to hang up in the eating area.	Have a drought in one part of the garden. What happens?	Discuss with the group that sometimes people don't have enough food. Then have a snack with only one serving per child. Afterward discuss: Did you want more? How did it feel not to be able to have more?	Share garden work.	Make breads together. Send home copies of recipes with all the children.
Music and Movement ⟶		Sing "The Garden Song" ("Inch by Inch") by Dave Mallet			
Fine Muscle ⟶	Cut out pictures of foods for mural.	Plant seeds.		Make a salad from garden produce to share with others.	Each child kneads a small amount of bread dough and adds it to class loaf.
Large Muscle ⟶		Cultivate the soil.			
Language ⟶	Discuss food groups and "balanced diet."	Discuss seeds to be sown. Contrast mature fruits and vegetables.		Discuss taking your portion of food and leaving enough for others.	Vocabulary— label food and put cans in categories. Make a grocery store.
Special Activities ⟶	Conduct a food drive this week. Ask families to bring in dried and canned foods to donate to a local food	Start a garden.	Problem-solve: We have one piece of watermelon and 4 children want it. What shall we do?		Pack up food with children to send to the food bank.

From *Discover the World: Empowering Young Children to Value Themselves, Others and the Earth.* Edited by Susan Hopkins and Jeffry Winters, Concerned Educators for a Safe Environment. New Society Publishers: Philadelphia PA, Santa Cruz, CA, and Gabriola Island BC; (800) 333-9093. Reprinted with permission.

Teaching Children About Cultural Diversity

Another area in which mealtime can be used to further children's global awareness is in regard to cultural diversity. It is one of the opportunities to nurture the development of enthusiasm, appreciation and respect for the differences as well as the similarities of all people.

Often, multi-cultural education is included in ways which, though unintended, might actually promote stereotypes and present incorrect information. For example, serving "ethnic" foods and presenting "ethnic" dances and music only on "ethnic" holidays may emphasize and misportray differences; showing pictures of cultural groups dressed in "traditional" clothing does not convey the reality of daily life, etc. This approach might also give the impression that all people of a particular cultural group do things in the same way.

The following guidelines, adapted from the book *Anti-Bias Curriculum: Tools for Empowering Young Children* by Louise Derman-Sparks and the Anti-Bias Curriculum Task Force, will help ensure that efforts to teach multi-cultural education at mealtime won't backfire:

❑ Prepare foods that children regularly eat at home. Include foods eaten by every child's family. Integrate culturally diverse cooking regularly at snack and lunch. Ask parents for recipes that you can include. (See *Cultural Appreciation Form* on pages 20–21.) Also, include foods from cultures not represented within the group.

❑ Don't stereotype. Be sure to avoid generalizations. Though certain foods may be traditionally identified with a particular cultural group, remember to point out that families within the same culture may eat differently from each other.

❑ Explain the difference between daily foods and holiday foods.

❑ Don't mix cultures up. Families from El Salvador do not eat the same foods as families from Mexico. Families recently from Mexico may not eat the same foods as third-generation Chicanos.

❏ Children may not like the new food they are supposed to be learning to appreciate. Teach children ways to decline food politely. Serve small portions and invite, but don't force them to try it. Help them understand that sometimes we like new things and sometimes we don't. If children make fun of the food or call a food "yucky," intervene immediately, explaining that it is not OK to respond in those ways, and offering other ways: "I've never tasted that before; what does it taste like?" or "It tastes different to me"; or, if a child really doesn't want to try, say "No, thank you; I don't want any today."

World Foods: Activity Chart

Concept ———→	Everyone eats.	There are many foods around the world that are similar.	Children need roots and identity.	Spices come from all over the world and change taste and smell.	People eat bread in many different forms.
Art Experience ———→	Collage with food pictures cut out from magazines.		Make a bread basket with white playdough by weaving designs over bread pan—bake.	Make a "spice circle." Children each share spice from home and glue on circle.	
Science Experience ———→	Eat something from each basic food group. Discuss taste, smell, and texture.	Make or buy and taste pancakes, won tons, tortillas, crepes. Compare. Discuss origins.	Taste many different kinds of breads from many ethnic sources.	Smell spice jars marked with pictures that represent home country, (curry-India, chili- So. America)	Observe and compare making yeast and unleavened breads.
Music and Movement ———→	Play games from Malvina Reynolds' album, *Artichoke, Griddle Cake and Other Good Things*.		Play "Stir Fry." Large "tape" circle on floor is "pan." Children hop in pan as they call out what food they are.		
Fine Muscle ———→	Cut out pictures of people marketing, preparing, and eating a variety of foods.	Prepare and eat foods of various cultures with appropriate utensils such as rice with chopsticks.		Push cloves into oranges to make pomander balls.	Stir, sift, knead, chop, etc.
Large Muscle ———→	Walk to store and buy an item from each food group.				Act out adding ingredients for bread. Add yeast and everyone rises.
Language ———→	Food Lotto. Make a set of cards representing many cultures.	Learn food names and associate with countries of origin.	Discuss kinds of food children eat at home— traditions from grandparents, etc.	Children share information about spice brought from home, how it is used in food, family traditions.	Learn bread names and associate with countries of origin.
Special Activities ———→	Set up a grocery store.		Have a "Festival of Breads." Parents bake bread and share culture and traditions.		Make various types of breads.

From *Discover the World: Empowering Young Children to Value Themselves, Others and the Earth*. Edited by Susan Hopkins and Jeffry Winters, Concerned Educators for a Safe Environment. New Society Publishers: Philadelphia PA, Santa Cruz CA, and Gabriola Island BC; (800) 333-9093. Reprinted with permission.

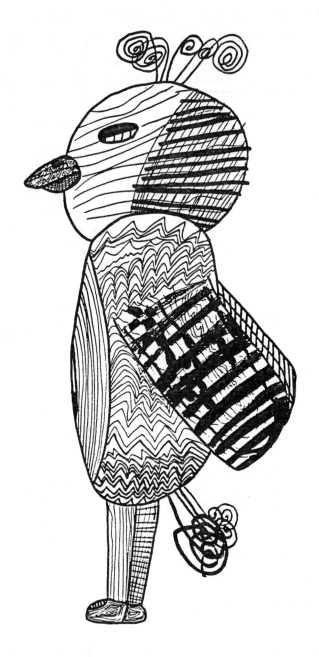

Cultural Appreciation Form

Here is a form which can be copied and sent home with the children to help you gather information about their cultural heritages. You can then refer to the forms and include experiences drawn from the customs and lifestyles of all of the children as you plan daily routines as well as special occasions.

Dear Parent,

We value diversity of cultures and family traditions and encourage you to enrich our program with your customs. With parents' help it is our goal to foster an awareness and appreciation of the world community.

Your Name _____

Child's Name _____

Principal Country(ies) of your family's heritage:

1. _____ 3. _____

2. _____ 4. _____

Please describe any family customs which are important to your family which would be helpful for us to be aware of, such as:

    Special foods your family eats.
    Eating utensils.
    Special clothing you wear.
    Special daily routines (stemming from your cultural background).
    Special words or cultural terms your family uses. Is another language spoken in your home? If yes, _____ .

Which holidays specific to your cultural heritage does your family celebrate which you would like us to be aware of?

Name of Holiday   Date(s)

1. _____ _____

2. _____ _____

3. _____ _____

4. _____ _____

Would you be willing to help us learn more about your family's heritage by (check all which apply):

[ ] Chatting with us informally about family customs/holidays.

[ ] Sending some cultural materials for us to use in working with the children, such as music, stories, foods, etc.

[ ] Visiting the program to help us teach the children more about your culture.

    Please include any other comments or information you wish to add and return with this form.

From *Discover the World: Empowering Young Children to Value Themselves, Others and the Earth*. Edited by Susan Hopkins and Jeffry Winters, Concerned Educators for a Safe Environment. New Society Publishers: Philadelphia PA, Santa Cruz CA, and Gabriola Island BC; (800) 333-9093. Reprinted with permission.

Children of the World: A Guided Fantasy

Guided fantasies can be a valuable tool for nurturing imagination, creativity and empathy. Through this type of creative visualization we can help children develop an appreciation for children all over the world. Here is an example for you to try. Feel free to adapt and simplify it to make it appropriate for your group. Soft music in the background can be added. Pause frequently as you speak, giving the children time to develop their images.

Start out by finding a comfortable position (either seated or lying down, where the children are not touching each other). *If, during the time we are doing this activity, you need to readjust your body to stay comfortable, feel free to quietly do so without bumping into anyone.*

Now, take a few deep breaths and close your eyes and imagine that you are about to begin a very special journey today. All of the children of the world will be getting together to become friends. Everyone is excited as they get ready for the event. From near and far children will be arriving at the magical land of the children. Imagine all the different ways that they could get there—by boat, by plane, by camel or elephant, by skateboard, bicycle, or roller skates, by walking or running. Imagine what other ways they might be arriving. How will you be arriving?

As the children begin to gather together, excitement fills the air. Look around and see all the friendly faces. What do the children look like? Where are they from? How are they dressed? How do you greet each other? Are you hearing languages that you've never heard before? How does everyone show their friendship though they speak so many different languages? Take a few moments to enjoy this time of meeting each other.

Soon all the children will gather together to share a meal. Everyone has brought one of their favorite foods to share. What food are you bringing to share? The children are seated at the largest table ever in the whole world. It is round so that everyone can see each other. It is decorated with dishes and ornaments from all over the world and is a wonderful sight to see.

When everyone is seated, begin to look around the table. See the amazing variety of foods! There are fruits and vegetables you have never seen before. There are hundreds of platters of foods being passed around the table. So many spices, so many colors—you had no idea there were so many different kinds of foods in the world. Smell the wonderful variety of smells. See the many ways that people eat—some with forks or spoons, some with chopsticks, some with their hands. Everyone is smiling and everyone is friendly and it's a wonderful feeling. You are learning that children around the world are both the same and different from each other. There are many ways of eating, many ways of speaking, and many ways to dress, but some things are the same everywhere. Everyone likes to smile and laugh and everyone likes to have friends.

At the end of the meal, many of the children are eagerly exchanging addresses and planning visits to each others' villages, cities, and countries. Deep in their hearts the children are beginning to believe that this kind of sharing and friendship is the thing that will help to make this world into the loving, peaceful place that everyone wants it to be. As you leave for home at the end of the day, you wave goodbye to all of your new friends.

Spend a few minutes thinking about your wonderful day and how lucky you are to have so many new friends from all over the world. When you are ready, slowly open your eyes and rest quietly until everyone else opens their eyes.

When you have completed the guided fantasy, invite children who wish to do so to share their experience with the group, or draw pictures about it.

Resources for Children: Cultural Diversity

The following publications for children address cultural diversity:

Bread• Bread • Bread by Ann Morris. New York: Lothrop, Lee, & Shepard Books, 1989. Beautiful pictures of people and the breads they eat, all around the world.

Families the World Over series. Lerner Publications, 241 First Avenue North, Minneapolis MN 55401. A beautiful series of photographic books showing the day-to-day lives of families around the world.

People by Peter Spier. New York: Doubleday, 1980. This book shows how people have so much in common, while showing how our diversity is reflected in the way we eat, celebrate holidays, play games, etc.

Skipping Stones. 80574 Hazelton Rd., Cottage Grove, OR 97424. (503) 942-9434. A multicultural children's quarterly magazine celebrating cultural diversity. Stories and poems submitted by children are printed in their original languages with accompanying English translations. Includes a guide for parents and teachers suggesting ways to integrate the ideas presented into everyday life.

Additional publications are listed in *Appendix B—Resources* on page 67.

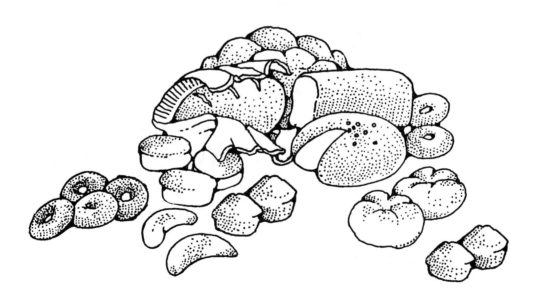

Handling Holidays and Special Occasions

Holidays almost always involve special foods, meals, cooking and baking. Often they also involve lots of excitement, high expectations from adults and children and a fair share of hard work and stress. For child care providers, they also include many questions such as: What do I expect of myself? What do I expect of the children? How can I involve the children and their families?

Some careful planning and evaluating can help you create celebrations which will leave you exuberant . . . instead of exhausted. Here is a checklist to help you evaluate your plans:

Expectations and Assumptions

___ What is your purpose in choosing to celebrate this holiday?

___ Are you planning activities automatically, just because you've always done them that way?

___ Are your plans based on what you really enjoy doing rather than on what you think the children or other adults expect you to do?

___ Are you making any automatic assumptions about what children will enjoy and understand?

___ Have you talked to the children about what would make the celebration special for them? Their hopes and ideas may be simpler than you think.

___ If you think the children have specific expectations, are they reasonable and agreeable with you?

"Age-appropriateness"

___ Are your plans appropriate for the level of development of the children who will be participating?

___ If there are children of mixed age range, are there activities that can be adapted to various ages so that everyone can participate?

___ How will the experience be meaningful for the children who will be participating?

___ What do you hope or think that the children will learn from the experience?

___ If cooking activities are a part of your plans, are they appropriate for the ages of the children who will be participating?

Cultural Awareness

___ Are your plans appropriate for the ethnic background of the children who will participate?

___ Are your holiday celebrations inclusive? Do they honor the cultural needs of all the families? Do they take into account that not everyone of the same ethnic background celebrates holidays in the same way?

___ What if some parents object to holiday celebrations? What kind of satisfactory alternatives will you provide for their children?

___ If you are including historical or cultural education in your celebration, have you checked to be sure that your information is accurate and does not promote stereotypes or perpetuate historical myths? (See *Native Americans and the Thanksgiving Holiday* on page 28.)

___ Will you explain to the children the differences between holidays and everyday life within cultures? If they will be seeing people dressed in festival costumes doing special dances and eating special holiday foods, will you also explain how this is different from the day-to-day life of the people?

"Elaborate-ness"

___ How elaborate do you expect the celebration to be?

___ Can you find creative alternatives to the bombardment of commercialism that surrounds the major holidays celebrated in the U.S.?

___ Are your plans simple enough so that the children won't feel overwhelmed?

___ Do your plans take the economic means of the children into account? If you plan to ask children to bring food or gifts, do you know that this won't create a hardship for anyone?

___ Do you have enough help? If not, who can you recruit to help you? Can you collaborate on a celebration with another child care program?

Health and Safety

___ Are you planning a healthful menu? Have you and the parents reached an agreement about an appropriate amount of sweets or other foods of questionable nutritional value?

___ Are materials used for decorations or in activities non-hazardous?

___ Are you using the same caution (regarding supervision and household safety) that you would on a day-to-day basis?

Note: Remember that you can choose whether or not to celebrate holidays. Other options could be to celebrate seasonal changes, birthdays, or special milestones for each child such as learning a new skill. Feel free to create your own special traditions and celebrations with and for the children that are meaningful, developmentally appropriate, healthy and fun.

Native Americans and the Thanksgiving Holiday

One example of distortion of history and culture connected with a holiday ritual involves Native Americans and the Thanksgiving holiday. Many of us recite the traditional tales about "the first Thanksgiving," unaware that this folklore alters historical facts and offends many Native Americans. The dramatization of the event conveys the impression that the natives were typically treated with respect and generosity. It rarely acknowledges the real impact of the settlers on the native population: that they disregarded and degraded their culture and took over their land. To Native Americans, Thanksgiving Day symbolizes the loss of their land, food, and culture.

If you wish to celebrate Thanksgiving, here are some resources to help you to plan activities that will be sensitive and meaningful to all children:

Anti-Bias Curriculum: Tools for Empowering Young Children by Louise Derman-Sparks and the A.B.C. Task Force, available from National Association for the Education of Young Children, 1834 Connecticut Ave., N.W., Washington, DC 20009-5786. Pages 87–90 deal specifically with the celebration of Thanksgiving.

Books Without Bias; Through Indian Eyes, and an excerpt from it *How to Tell the Difference: A Checklist for Evaluating Native American Children's Books* by Beverly Slapin, Doris Seale and Rosemary Gonzales are available from Oyate, 2702 Mathews Street, Berkeley, CA 94702. These are both critiques of current children's literature about Native Americans and guides to literature written by Native Americans and others which the editors found free of stereotypes.

Daybreak Star Reach, a monthly children's paper with poems, stories, and drawings by Native American children from all cultures, is available through United Indians of All Tribes Foundation, Discovery Park, P.O. Box 99100, Seattle, WA 98199. (206) 285-4425. Curriculum and books about Native Americans are also available.

The People of the Breaking Day by Marcia Sewall, New York: Atheneum, 1990. Describes everyday life in a Wampanoag/Naragansett village during a typical year before the Pilgirms arrived.

Where Does Food Come From?

Children who live on a farm may learn through their daily life experience about where their food comes from. For other children it will take a variety of experiences for them to realize that food doesn't magically appear on their plate or even in the grocery store. Here are some suggestions of things to do to help children learn that many people work hard in the long, step-by-step process that eventually brings the food to their table.

❑ Plan field trips to places where food is grown, processed, sold and cooked: a farmer's market, plant nursery, orchard, farm, food processing factory, supermarket, corner grocery store, commercial kitchen, restaurant; or go on a guided tour of the kitchen in your own child care center or family day care home.

❑ Display posters representing the workers who participated along the path that our food takes: farmers, factory workers, truck drivers, grocery store clerks, cooks, etc. Provide magazine pictures for making collages showing the people who help to bring us our food. Select posters that do not perpetuate racial or sexual stereotypes.

- Invite parents who work in food-related jobs to come as visitors and talk about what they do.
- Refer to *Gardening With Children* on page 33.
- Here are some books that talk about where food comes from:

The American Family Farm. A Photo Essay by George Ancona with text by Joan Anderson. San Diego, CA: Harcourt Brace Jovanovich Publishers, 1989. Visits to three very different farming families.

Bananas—from Manolo to Margie by George Ancona. New York: Clarion Books, 1982. Through photographs and text, readers follow bananas from a banana plantation in Honduras to the United States, and meet the many people who play a part in the journey.

- and a board game for school-age children:

Back to the Farm. Available from Animal Town Cooperative Ventures, P.O. Box 485, Healdsburg, CA 95448. 1-800-445-8642.

Helping Children Become Smart Consumers

The food industry in this country spends over six billion dollars a year influencing children through advertising. Parents, especially those who are tired and overworked, are particularly vulnerable to being influenced by persistent offspring to purchase foods that have less than ideal nutritional value. When children learn to be discriminating consumers themselves, parents will be less likely to face these power struggles. Here are some suggestions as to how you might educate children to become smart consumers:

❏ Plan a food shopping trip with school-age children, in which they are included in the entire process—meal planning, list making, selection of brands, label reading, shopping cart pushing, and unpacking and putting the food away. This will offer opportunities for discussion about checking expiration dates on labels, comparing prices, careful storage of foods which need to be frozen and refrigerated (they need to be put away as soon as you get home), selecting products which are packaged with ecology in mind, the comparisons between canned, frozen and fresh foods, and on and on. Encourage younger children to help you in any way that is appropriate, and talk aloud as you compare prices and read labels. They will be learning a lot just by listening to you.

❏ Have the children tally the number of commercials during an hour of Saturday morning television. Ask the following questions:

- How many were for food items?
- How many were for nutritious food items? How do you know?
- Why do you think they were shown during children's programs?
- Do you think that everything the ads said was true? If not, why not?
- If not, does that bother you?

❏ At the grocery store, compare sizes and prices of a particular
product, such as frozen corn. Are all sizes and brands the
same price? How do they vary? How can you determine
which is the best bargain? Compare packaged mixes to fresh
foods. Read some labels. Are there some unfamiliar words?
How do they decide in what order to list the ingredients?
(See *Appendix C—How to Get the Most Information from a
Product Label,* page 75.) When packages say "natural," "lite,"
etc., what does that mean—if anything? How can you find
out? Compare the calories, fat or sugar content in three of
your favorite snack foods. Compare packaging of different
brands of the same type of food. Which company used the
most wasteful packaging? Which used the least? (See
Appendix D—Think of Mother Earth When You're Shopping,
page 79.)

Consumer Reports has a magazine designed to help children (8–14 years)
become wise consumers:

Zillions: Consumer Reports for Kids. Box 51777, Boulder, CO 80321-1177

Gardening with Children

One of the most exciting and enjoyable ways to teach children about where food comes from is through gardening activities. Even toddlers love to participate—they can fill pots with dirt, chop up dirt clods with child-size tools, and water plants with a sprinkling can or a garden hose turned on low. If you don't have a garden area, you can start with an egg carton, some soil and a windowsill.

When children plant vegetable or fruit seeds and watch them grow, they are learning many things, such as:

- ❑ Food does not start out at the grocery store.
- ❑ Some of our food comes from the earth.
- ❑ Plants need soil, water and sunlight.
- ❑ Plants have seeds, roots and leaves.
- ❑ There are seasons and life cycles.
- ❑ Plants are living things and need to be cared for.
- ❑ I can grow some of my own food.
- ❑ Seeds that I find in my fruits and vegetables can be planted to grow more fruits and vegetables.

Children who successfully plant and grow their own food will feel pride in their accomplishment and can develop respect for nature and for their surroundings. They may even be more willing to taste a new vegetable if they've grown it themselves.

Here are some planting activities that are fun to do with children. The more they can do independently, the more they are likely to learn.

❑ Grow mung bean, alfalfa, or other edible sprouts in a jar:

1. Soak about a tablespoon of seeds overnight in a jar of water. Cover the mouth of the jar with cheesecloth secured with a rubber band.

2. In the morning, drain the water off and set the jar in a cool, dark place.

3. Rinse and drain them at least twice daily for about four to five days. Talk with the children about the changes they notice each day.

4. If you are growing sprouts in a child care center, and no one will be around on the weekend to keep them moist, start the sprouts on a Monday.

5. Place the jar in the sunlight for a few hours to let the chlorophyll form.

6. When the leaves have turned green, the sprouts are ready to eat. Now the children can use them in sandwiches or salads.

❏ Grow a baby citrus tree:

1. Have the children save seeds from an orange, tangerine, lemon or grapefruit and soak them overnight.

2. Provide the children with individual containers for planting (egg cartons, milk cartons, peat pots—just be sure to make drainage holes to prevent the seeds from rotting) and let them fill their containers with good potting soil.

3. Have each child plant 2 or 3 seeds about 1 inch deep in their container. (Have some rulers on hand to talk about how deep 1 inch is.)

4. Have the children keep them in a warm sunny spot, water them as the soil begins to feel dry, and watch for the seeds to sprout.

❏ Grow a vegetable:

1. Follow the steps for planting citrus seeds, but use vegetable seeds. Beans or peas are good choices because they sprout quickly and grow fast.

2. When the seedlings are big enough, if you have an outdoor garden, the children can transplant them.

❏ Provide the children with some large seeds such as beans or peas and let them sprout the seeds in wet paper towels or cotton in a transparent container. This will enable the children to watch the whole process and have a better idea of what's going on under the soil.

❏ When you are involved in planting activities with children, their learning can be enhanced by asking questions and encouraging experiments such as these:

• What's inside a seed?

• Does it have a top and a bottom?

• If we plant seeds in different directions will the roots and leaves still know which way to grow?

• What does a seed need in order to grow?

- Let the children study plants and seeds under a magnifying glass.
- Let the children experiment by planting in different soils, under varying lighting conditions and temperatures, with more or less water, etc.
- Compare and discuss the results.

- Measure daily or weekly growth of plants and keep a chart or graph.
- Do all seeds grow at the same speed? Compare the growth of beans or peas to the growth of an avocado seed.

As much as possible, let the children discover their own answers to these questions.

❏ Learn the names of the parts of plants. (You can cut out flannel board pieces to show the parts that grow above and below the ground—seeds or bulbs, roots, leaves, stems, buds and flowers.) Then talk about the different parts of plants that we eat—e.g., carrots and potatoes are roots, broccoli and cauliflower are flowers, lettuce and spinach are leaves, celery and asparagus are stems.

❏ Have the children save the seeds from the fruits and vegetables they eat. They can cut out pictures of the foods from magazines and make charts showing which food grows from which seed.

❏ According to the ages of the children, your own interest in gardening and the space that is available, gardening activities can be more extensive. Older children can research, plan and develop an entire vegetable garden. Work with them to decide what needs to be done, how to divide up the work, etc.

Here are some good books about gardening with children:

Linnea's Windowsill Garden by Christina Bjork and Lena Anderson, Translated by Joan Sandin, R&S Books, Stockholm, 1988.

Gardens for Growing People: A Guide to Gardening With Children by Ruth Kantor Lopez, Gardens for Growing People, CA, 1990.

Kids Gardening: A Kids' Guide to Messing Around in the Dirt by Kevin Raftery and Kim Gilbert Raftery, Klutz Press, Palo Alto, 1989.

The Garden Book by Wes Porter, A Somerville House Book, Workman Publisher, New York, NY 10003, 1990.

The Growing Seeds: A Guided Fantasy

Here is a guided fantasy for children who are participating in planting activities. Playing a tape of soft music or sounds of nature will enhance the experience. Adapt it to a longer or shorter version depending on the age and attention span of the children. Pause between sentences to give the children time to visualize.

First curl up into a comfortable little ball. Now, close your eyes and pretend that you are a tiny seed being planted in the ground and covered gently by rich fertile soil. Keep your eyes closed and curl up as small as you can.

Now, imagine that it's early morning and you are beginning to feel the warmth of the sun on the soil. You feel warm and cozy as the sun comes up. Soon someone comes along with a sprinkling can and gently waters all of the little seeds. (The adult can walk around the room gently patting heads to feel like water drops.) *Take a deep breath and enjoy the smell of the moist earth.*

Notice how the water keeps you cool and damp through the hot afternoon sun. Before long it is evening, and then, night.

Now imagine the next day…and the next night…and another day…and another night…and slowly, very slowly, you feel your seed covering begin to open as your tiny roots reach down into the soil. Then your stem and leaves begin to reach up and out towards the sun. You are happy because you have had just enough sunshine and water to help you grow. (Suggest they begin to unfold and reach up, gradually stretching up to standing position.) *When you have stretched your stem and leaves up as tall as you can, take a deep breath of clean, fresh air, and stop and think about what kind of plant you have grown into. When you are ready, open your eyes and stand or sit quietly until all of the other seeds have finished sprouting.*

You might then encourage the children to talk about their experiences and what kind of plants they became. They may also wish to draw pictures based on their seed-growing fantasy.

Where Do the Leftovers Go?

Does our garbage just disappear? If not, what happens to it? Here are some activities that will help the children learn the answers.

- ❑ Save food scraps (other than meat products) and use them to make compost. See page 44 for instructions on making your compost pile.

- ❑ Do a "planting" experiment to find out what biodegradable means. Bury a variety of items in the soil—an apple core, a glass bottle, a styrofoam cup, some fallen leaves, etc. Dig them up every week or so for a month to see which ones change and which ones do not. Discuss the results.

- ❑ Make recycled paper: Tear up scrap paper or newspaper into tiny pieces and add them to a large pan with enough warm water to cover them. Stir and moosh them around until they become mushy. Slip a piece of wire mesh screening into the pan and lift it up, gathering some of the paper mixture and letting the water drain through. Cover with another piece of screen and blot heavily with a large sponge, removing as much water as possible. Gently turn it out onto a dry newspaper and let it dry overnight. Use the homemade paper for an art activity.

- ❑ Go on field trips to a garbage dump and a recycling center.

- ❑ Do a cleanup at the park and see how much food packaging litter you find.

- ❑ Do a one-day study of household garbage with older children. Sort it by type and weigh and measure it at the end of the day. How much is recyclable; how much isn't. How much came from packaging? How much can go in the compost? Make a chart to record results. Compare one day to another. See how much you can reduce a day's garbage with some planning.

- ❑ Do a study of leftover food garbage only. After a meal, collect, sort, and evaluate the leftover food. How much of each item was uneaten? Not all waste is the result of people's carelessness. Food waste studies can open dialogue between adults and children to find out why certain foods are not being eaten. The results may be surprising—children may be uncomfortable in their eating environment, they may be in a hurry to get to recess, or they may just not like the meatloaf recipe!

Here are some books about what happens to garbage:

Going Green: A Kid's Handbook to Saving the Planet by J. Elkington, J. Hailes, D. Hill, and J. Makower, Puffin Books, 1990.

Garbage! Where It Comes From, Where It Goes by Evan and Janet Hadingham, Simon & Schuster, New York, 1990.

Making Everyone a Part of Your Recycling Plan

Whether its in the home or in the child care setting, establishing a recycling program works best if everyone is involved. Adults can take responsibility for gathering or purchasing necessary supplies and transporting wastes to the recycling center, older children can help with research, planning, set-up and maintenance of the program. Younger children can help by decorating boxes to use as storage containers and helping to decide where to keep them and by sorting recyclables.

Here are some ideas to help you establish a successful recycling program:

❑ Find out what local recycling programs are available in your community (see page 43 for state recycling phone numbers) and find out what items can be recycled.

❑ If you do not have a curbside pick-up program in your community, decide on a practical schedule for going to the recycling center.

❑ Decide on the most convenient place(s) to store the recyclables—kitchen, garage, back porch, closet, etc. If you don't have lots of space in a nearby, convenient spot (e.g., kitchen), use small containers there and, when full, empty them into larger bins in an outside storage area (e.g., basement). The more convenient your system, the quicker you will adapt to using it.

❑ Select containers, preferably with handles or on wheels, that won't be too heavy or bulky to carry when they fill up. Some possible choices: sturdy cardboard cartons, paper grocery bags, empty milk crates, plastic laundry baskets, rattan baskets, or recycling storage units specially designed for the purpose. (See *Appendix B—Resources* for places to order these.)

❑ As they accumulate, sort your recyclable items into the containers to be set out for curbside pick-up or delivered to the recycling center.

❑ If you have a yard, establish a compost for recycling food waste (other than meat products) and other organic materials.*

❑ Be creative about recycling items that can't be taken to the recycling center. Clothes and household goods that are in useable condition can be donated to non-profit organizations. Many items are usable for arts, crafts and science projects with children. A current fashion trend is jewelry, art pieces and clothing made of recycled material—a sign of the times!

❑ If there is no recycling program in your community, join with other concerned residents and get one started. *The Recycler's Handbook: Simple Things You Can Do* by The Earthworks Group will tell you how to begin.

*To learn more about composting turn to page 44.

State Recycling Phone Numbers and Recycling Hotlines

Environmental Defense Fund
1-800-225-5333

Alabama: 205-271-7700
Alaska: 907-465-2666
Arizona: 602-255-3303
Arkansas: 501-562-7444
California: 916-323-3508
Colorado: 303-320-8333
Connecticut: 203-566-8895
Delaware: 302-736-5742
District of Columbia: 202-767-8512
Florida: 904-488-0300
Georgia: 404-656-3898
Idaho: 208-334-2789
Illinois: 217-782-6761
Indiana: 317-232-8883
Iowa: 515-281-3426
Kansas: 913-296-1500
Kentucky: 502-564-6716
Louisiana: 504-342-1216
Maine: 207-289-2111
Maryland: 301-974-3291
Massachusetts: 617-292-5962
Michigan: 517-373-0540
Minnesota: 612-296-8439
Minnesota: 612-536-0816
Mississippi: 601-961-5171

Missouri: 314-751-3176
Montana: 406-444-2821
Nebraska: 402-471-4210
Nevada: 702-885-4420
New Hampshire: 603-224-6996
New Jersey: 201-648-1978
New Mexico: 505-827-2780
New York: 518-457-7336
North Carolina: 919-733-7015
North Dakota: 701-224-2366
Ohio: 614-265-6353 or 614-644-2917
Oklahoma: 405-271-7519
Oregon: 503-229-5826
Pennsylvania: 717-787-7382
South Dakota: 605-773-3153
Tennessee: 615-741-3424
Texas: 512-458-7271
Utah: 801-538-6170
Vermont: 802-244-8702
Virginia: 804-786-8679
Washington, DC: 202-939-7116
West Virginia: 304-348-3370
Wisconsin: 608-267-7565
Wyoming: 307-777-7752

State Recycling Hotlines

Alabama: 1-800-392-1924
California: 1-800-RECYCAL
Colorado: 1-800-438-8800
Delaware: 1-800-CASHCAN
Maryland: 1-800-345-BIRP
Minnesota: 1-800-592-9528
New Jersey: 1-800-492-4242

Ohio: 1-800-282-6040
Rhode Island: 1-800-RICLEAN
Tennessee: 1-800-342-4038
Texas: 1-800-CLEANTX
Virginia: 1-800-KEEPITT
Washington: 1-800-RECYCLE

Source: *The Green Lifestyle Handbook,* Jeremy Rifkin, Editor, Henry Holt & Company, New York,1990

Building a Compost Heap

Composting is a great way to help children learn the benefits of recycling organic garbage. The size of your compost will depend on how much space you have.

What to Do

❑ Choose an out-of-the-way spot in your yard, preferably a level, well-drained, sunny spot, but a shady one will work too. A 3' × 3' plot is a good size to retain heat and compost faster, but use whatever size space you have. *If you don't have a large enough dirt area, you can use a planter box.*

❑ A simple compost bin can be enclosed with chicken wire fencing formed into a cylinder or into a square by attaching it to four metal or wood posts.

❑ Line the bottom with moist peat moss, shredded paper, leaves or grass clippings. Sprinkle lightly with water as you add the layers.

❑ Buy some earthworms at a local nursery or bait shop and put them into the compost mixture. Their continual tunneling helps to build rich and fertile soil and insure a successful compost.

❏ As you accumulate them, keep adding any food scraps (other than meat or dairy products) and other organic substances such as wood chips or garden clippings. High nitrogen substances such as blood meal, bone meal and manure can also be added to speed up the decaying process.

❏ Turn the mixture with a pitchfork or shovel every few days. Keep food scraps covered with grass clipping, dirt or leaves to avoid flies.

❏ Talk with the children about the changes taking place as you tend the compost together. Observe the worms at work. They're fun to watch and can help children learn respect for the value of all living things and the jobs they do.

❏ When the compost is broken down and ready to use, usually in two to eight weeks, dig in with the children and add your new "homemade" soil to the vegetable garden, around bushes and trees and to potted plants. If you sift it, you can use it as a planting mixture for sprouting garden seeds.

CHAPTER THREE

Activities for Kids

What Children Learn Through Cooking Activities

Cooking is an ideal vehicle for nutrition education for young children. It allows them to become familiar with foods they might not otherwise see, and often children will eagerly eat foods which they have prepared, even when they refused them previously. Cooking activities also allow children to share the process of working toward a goal and sharing the fruits of their labors with friends and family.

Cooking develops many concepts and skills, including:

Motor Skills:	Scrubbing, tearing, dipping
	Pouring, mixing, shaking, spreading
	Rolling, kneading, juicing, peeling
	Cutting, grating, slicing
Language Arts:	Naming—foods, actions, equipment, processes, categories
	Comparisons
	Time designations
	Following directions
	Letter/word recognition
Mathematics:	Measuring
	Counting
	Sequencing
	Classification
	Numbers on tags and labels

Socialization:	Sharing
	Teamwork
	Self-care
	Cultural food habits
	Food-related professions in the community
Science:	Heat and coolness
	Floating
	Dissolving
	Evaporation
	Browning
	Leavening
	Melting
	Gelatinization
	Sense awareness

Survival Guide to Cooking With Children

The 5 Laws of Successful Cooking Projects

1. Plan projects at the childrens' level of development (see below).

2. Keep your participation in the project to a minimum but supervise constantly.

3. Plan cooking activities to fit within the day's menu of nutritious foods.

4. Insist upon good safety practices and have a first aid kit handy.

5. Insist that the children help with cleanup.

Remember That Food Handling Skills Develop Over Time[1]

2-year-olds   ***Big Arm Muscles***
Scrub
Tear-Break-Snap
Dip

3-year-olds   ***Medium Muscles / Hands***
Wrap
Pour
Mix
Shake
Spread

4-year-olds   ***Small Muscles / Fingers***
Peel
Roll
Juice
Crack eggs
Mash

5 and up   ***Fine Coordination / Working Against Resistance***
Measure
Cut
Grind
Beat with egg beater

Single-Portion Cooking

Two main approaches to children's cooking projects are commonly used in group settings. One is giving each child a task that contributes to making a finished product that everyone will eat. The other is single-portion cooking, sometimes called "cup cooking."

The advantage of the former is that it allows a child the cooperative experience of cooking and generally requires less setup time. However, it's sometimes difficult for the adult in charge to ensure that everyone keeps interested, and it isn't always clear to the child how his or her task related to the outcome.

Single-portion cooking lets the child participate in the cooking process each step of the way. It also conveys the idea that (at least sometimes) "if you don't work, you don't eat," a handy notion for children to keep in mind as they grow up. And for the squeamish, it requires the child to touch only her own food. It does take considerably more advance preparation to cook this way, and some recipes or equipment don't lend themselves easily to this method. But we highly recommend giving the technique a try.

The general idea here is to set up a number of work stations that correspond to specific steps within a recipe. Generally a picture illustrating the directions for the step would be placed behind the tools and ingredients a child would need to complete the step. The child should move systematically through the "stations" with little (or no) adult help. The pictures should illustrate every task, starting with handwashing and ending with eating (and cleanup if a picture helps!).

On the next page is an example of how our recipe for Peanut Butter Ping-Pong Balls would look in single portion format. Don't let what you feel is a lack of drawing talent deter you from trying this with other recipes!

PEANUT BUTTER PING PONG BALLS

① Wash Hands

② Add to Bowl — 2 T. Peanut Butter

③ Add — 1 T. Honey

④ Add — ⅛ t. Vanilla

⑤ Add — ¾ cup { crispy rice cereal

⑥ Roll into balls

⑦ Refrigerate 1 hr.

⑧ Eat!

If you would like to convert a favorite recipe into a single-portion cooking project, we have some advice for you:

❏ Think through the logistics of the project. Will all of the steps work in individual bowls or containers? Do you have the equipment for each step?

❏ Rather than have the children measuring out miniscule amounts of herbs, spices, or other ingredients, you may want to make up a "spice mixture" or "flour mixture."

❏ Convert your recipe to single portions by division. For example, if your recipe calls for 2 cups of flour, and you want 8 portions, it's probably easiest to first convert the cups to tablespoons: 2 cups = 32 tablespoons. Then divide by the number of servings: 32 tablespoons ÷ 8 = 4 tablespoons per portion. You may find the table of measurements in *Appendix E*, page 81 helpful. If you end up with some intimidating fraction, you can often combine ingredients, as in the "spice mixture" example above, or change the portion size (like making the recipe serve 8 instead of 10).

❏ *Do a trial run before you attempt the recipe with children.* You want them to feel successful.

The book *Cook and Learn, Pictorial Single Portion Recipes* (Beverly Veitch and Thelma Harms, Addison-Wesley Publishing Company, Menlo Park, 1981) is an excellent guide (with recipes) to the single-portion cooking method.

Books We Especially Like for Children

There are of course, thousands of wonderful books for children. Some, however, are more useful than others for conveying positive nutrition messages. The list below is by no means exhaustive, but we have found these books to be both appropriate in content and readily available.

Primarily Picture Books . . .

Bread•Bread•Bread. Ann Morris. New York: Lothrop, Lee, & Shepard Books, 1989. Beautiful pictures of people and the breads they eat, all around the world.

Families the World Over series. Minneapolis: Lerner Publications. Everyday life, including family mealtimes, in many cultures.

Eating the Alphabet: Fruits and Vegetables from A to Z. Lois Ehlert. San Diego: Harcourt Brace Jovanovich, 1989.

Growing Vegetable Soup. Lois Ehlert. San Diego: Harcourt Brace Jovanovich, 1987.

What's on My Plate. Ruth Belov Gross. Illustrations by Isadore Seltzer. New York: Macmillan Publishing Company, 1990. Food origins are presented in this beautifully illustrated book.

Strawberry. Jennifer Coldroy and George Bernard. Englewood Cliffs, NJ: Silver Burdett Press, 1988. (Also: *Bean & Plant, Chicken & Egg, Mushroom, Potato*). These books trace the life cycles of a variety of foodstuffs.

My Five Senses. Aliki. New York: Harper & Row, Publishers, 1989.

The Carrot Seed. Ruth Krauss. New York : Harper & Row, Publishers, 1945.

The Very Hungry Caterpillar. Eric Carle. Philomel Books, 1987.

The Pigs' Alphabet. Leah Palmer Preiss. Boston: David R. Goding, Publisher, 1990. Two pigs eat their way through a menu from A to Z, with predict able results.

Happy Veggies. Mayumi Oda. Berkeley: Parallax Press, 1988.

More Challenging Reading . . .

Winnie-the-Pooh: A Tight Squeeze. A.A. Milne. Wisconsin: Golden Press Company, 1976. What happens when a bear eats too much!

Bread and Jam for Frances. Russell Hoban. New York: Harper & Row, Publishers, 1964. Frances announces that she will only eat bread and jam, and she gets an opportunity to try just that!

The Berenstain Bears and Too Much Junk Food. Stan and Jan Berenstain. New York: Random House, 1985.

The Berenstain Bears Forget Their Manners. Stan and Jan Berenstain. New York: Random House, 1985.

A Medieval Feast. Aliki. New York: Harper & Row, Publishers, 1983. This exquisitely illustrated book describes preparations for a kingly feast during the Middle Ages.

Pancakes for Breakfast. Tomie dePaola. San Diego: Harcourt Brace Jovanovich, 1978.

Stone Soup. Marcia Brown. New York: Macmillan Publishing Company, 1986. Cooperative soup-making.

Chicken Soup with Rice. Maurice Sendak. New York: Scholastic Book Service, 1962.

Green Eggs and Ham. Dr. Seuss. New York: Beginners Books, 1960.

Gregory, the Terrible Eater. M. Sharmat. New York: Scholastic Book Service, 1980.

How My Parents Learned to Eat. Ina R. Friedman. Boston: Houghton Mifflin, Publishers, 1984. A bi-cultural look at eating customs.

Manners. Aliki. New York: Greenwillow Books, 1990. A humorous look at good manners.

Let's Play Farm, Grocery Store, Restaurant . . .

After children have been on field trips to food production or distribution facilities, or after they've read books about the people who work to make food available for them, they often enjoy pretending that they are involved in these roles. It's a lot of fun to set up role-playing environments for children, and you will find that much of the equipment can be obtained quite inexpensively by asking friends or the children's parents for usable items, or by combing through thrift shops and flea markets.

Grocery Store
Activities: buying, taking home, storing, cooking, eating food

Materials: food boxes, cans, etc.
              shopping cart or baskets, grocery bags, "money"
              cash register
              shelves, table, refrigerator, stove, sink

Truck Drivers
Activities: loading and unloading boxes of food
              driving trucks

Materials: truck drivers' uniforms
              clipboards
              "trucks"
              boxes or blocks

Farmers
Activities: spading, planting, watering, hoeing, harvesting
              caring for animals

Materials: play area (preferably with dirt!)
              buckets or watering cans
              shovel, trowel, hoe
              empty seed packets
              fruit and vegetable models, baskets
              "farm animals"

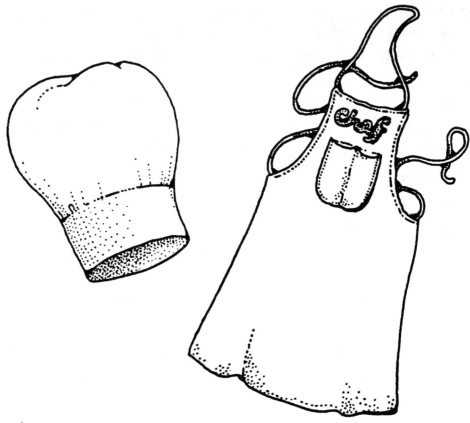

Restaurant

Activities: preparing food for "customers," providing service to customers, ordering from menus, settling bills

Materials: trays

tableware, placemats, tablecloths

cash register and play money

order pads and pencils

aprons, hats

menus (you can make these by laminating pictures of food onto lightweight cardboard, or have the children make them up using pictures or words)

play food

food preparation equipment (play stove, sink, pots and pans, etc. . . .)

Smelly Boxes and Feelie Socks

This activity is a fun way for young children to learn about the sensory characteristics of foods. It requires them to play detective, identifying foods using only one clue (sense) at a time.

Feelie Socks (Touch)

Place sturdy foods inside clean socks. Ask the children to put their hands into the socks and identify the foods only by touch. Talk with them about how the foods feel. Are they smooth, bumpy, fuzzy? Are they round, irregular, long, large, or small?

Smelly Boxes (Smell)

Place strong smelling foods inside opaque plastic containers with lids. Make slits in the lids (as in a piggy bank). Ask the children to identify the foods by smell alone. Ideas: lemons, onions, garlic, tuna, cotton balls saturated with vanilla.

Can You Believe Your Ears? (Hearing)

Ask the children to close their eyes and identify foods using only the sense of hearing. Examples: popcorn popping, soda water fizzing, apples or carrots crunching.

Mystery Solutions (Taste)

Stir flavoring agents (below) into plain water. Give each child four spoons to dip into the solutions for tiny tastes.

Sweet: sugar
Salty: salt
Sour: white vinegar
Bitter: unsweetened grapefruit juice

Reach for the Riddles

Children love guessing games. You can use riddles, either read aloud or on flash cards, to communicate nutrition concepts or help young children learn to identify foods. Clues can be given that:

❑ describe a food by color, size, shape, or taste

❑ ask for rhyming words

❑ ask for words that begin with certain letters

We'll give you a few examples and let you make up your own riddles. You can also have the children make up riddles for each other!

I'm orange and long.
I rhyme with "parrot."
I grow in the ground.
I'm a __(carrot)_____.

I have four legs.
And I say "moo."
I eat grass and make
Yummy milk for you.
What am I? (cow)

Now it's your turn!

_____   _____

_____   _____

_____   _____

_____   _____

_____   _____

_____   _____

_____   _____

_____   _____

_____   _____

_____   _____

Some Simple Silly Songs to Sing

Here are some simple songs about the topics in this book which we have composed to sing with preschool children. We put them to the tunes of familiar songs and nursery rhymes, so that you would be able to learn them easily. You and the children can have great fun adding original verses or composing your own songs. Use familiar melodies or make them up.

The Vegetable Song

To the tune of: Twinkle, Twinkle, Little Star

Carrots, peas and broccoli,
Vegetables are good for me.
For my snack and in my lunch,
Veggie sticks are great to munch.
Carrots, peas and broccoli,
Vegetables are good for me.

The Good Food Song*

To the tune of: Old MacDonald Had a Farm

Vegetables are good for me,
EE I EE I O
And so I eat them happily,
EE I EE I O
(Children take turns naming vegetables
  they like)
With a carrot, carrot, here
And a carrot, carrot there
Here a carrot there a carrot,
Everywhere a carrot, carrot.
Vegetables are good for me,
EE I EE I O

Fruits are very good for me
EE I EE I O.
And so I eat them happily,
EE I EE I O.
(Children take turns naming fruits
  they like)
With an apple, apple here
And an apple, apple there
Here an apple, there an apple,
Everywhere an apple, apple
Fruits are very good for me
EE I EE I O.

Brush, Brush, Brush Your Teeth

To the Tune of: Row, Row, Row Your Boat

Brush, Brush, Brush Your Teeth,
'til they're shiny bright,
They'll be healthy, they'll be strong,
If you treat them right.

Oh, Before I Eat My Meals

*To the Tune of: If You're Happy and You
  Know It Clap Your Hands.
  (Pantomime the actions)*

Oh, before I eat my meals I wash my hands,
    (scrub, scrub)
Oh, before I eat my meals I wash my hands,
    (scrub, scrub)
Oh, it's very smart, I think,
Sends those germs right down the sink.
Oh, before I eat my meals I wash my hands,
    (scrub, scrub)
Oh, before I eat my meals I set my place
    (set, set)
Oh, before I eat my meals I set my place,
    (set,set)
I set everything I need,
I feel very proud, indeed.
Oh, before I eat my meals I set my place,
    (set,set)
Oh, before I eat my meals I pass the food,
    (pass the plate)
Oh, before I eat my meals I pass the food,
    (pass the plate)
'Cause we know it's only fair
For us all to have our share
Oh, before I eat my meals I pass the food,

*Use your own creativity to add other categories. Some possibilities: grains, breads, proteins, cheese, soups, etc.

The More That We Recycle

To the tune of: Did You Ever See a Lassie Go This Way and That?

Oh, the more that we recycle, recycle,
  recycle,
Oh, the more that we recycle,
The happier we'll be.
'Cause your earth is my earth
And my earth is your earth
So the more that we recycle
The happier we'll be.

When We Eat Together

To the tune of: Here We Go 'Round the Mulberry Bush
(Pantomime the actions)

This is the way we pass the plate,
Pass the plate, pass the plate,
This is the way we pass the plate
When we eat together.

And this is the way we use our fork,
Use our fork, use our fork,
This is the way we use our fork,
When we eat together.

And this is the way we pour our juice [or
  milk]
Pour our juice, pour our juice,
This is the way we pour our juice
When we eat together.

This is the way we cut our food,
Cut our food, cut our food,
This is the way we cut our food,
When we eat together.

This is the way we clear our place,
Clear our place, clear our place.
This is the way we clear our place,
When we eat together.
(Make up and add your own verses or have the children make up their own.)

A Recycling Song

To the tune of: Frere Jacques

Save your bottles, save your bottles,
Save your cans, Save your cans
Bundle up your papers, bundle up your
  papers,
That's the plan, that's the plan.

A Planting Song

To the tune of: Mary Had a Little Lamb
[When you are doing a planting activity, use the names of the children in the group in place of "Mary"]

[Mary] had a little seed,
Little seed, little seed,
[Mary] had a little seed,
And hoped that it would grow.

She watered it and pulled the weeds,
Pulled the weeds, pulled the weeds,
She watered it and pulled the weeds
With sprinkling can and hoe.

And every day the sun would shine,
Sun would shine, sun would shine,
And every day the sun would shine
And warm it for a while.

And soon a little sprout came out,
Sprout came out, sprout came out,
And soon a little sprout came out
It made dear [Mary] smile.

A lettuce plant began to grow,
Began to grow, began to grow.
A lettuce plant began to grow,
So fresh and crisp and green.

Then carefully she picked some leaves,
Picked some leaves, picked some leaves.
Then carefully she picked some leaves,
And rinsed them nice and clean.

Now homegrown salad, she will eat,
She will eat, she will eat.
Now homegrown salad she will eat.
She grew a healthy treat.

One Small Planet

Written by Jon Fromer

We've got to keep the waters pure,
We've got to keep the mountains high,
And make sure the birds keep flying
In the clear blue sky.
'Cause we've got . . . chorus

There's only so much water,
There's only so much land,
There's only so much air to breathe,
Let's keep it clean while we can,
'Cause we've got . . . chorus

Chorus: One small planet
With a lot of people
It's all we've got so let's take care.
One small world for us to live in,
It's all we have, so we've got to
share.

Suggested Songs

The following children's songs related to food, nutrition and ecology can be found in the songbook, *Rise Up Singing,* edited by Peter Blood-Patterson, and available from Sing Out Corporation, PO Box 5253, Bethlehem, PA 18015. (215) 865-5366. The book includes the words and chords to these songs, as well as references to recordings on which they can be found:

Aiken Drum   **Garbage**
Apple Picker's Reel   **The Garden Song**
Biscuits in the Oven   **Little Blue Top**
The Bread Song   **Oats, Peas, Beans & Barley**
Brush Your Teeth   **On Top of Spaghetti**
Down on the Farm   **Peanut Butter**
The Earth Is My Mother **Pollution**

. . . and more!

Just for Fun

This menu is an exact replica of one written by Jacki as an already nutrition-conscious 9 year old (though perhaps a bit heavy on the red meat!). School-age children can have a great time devising their own unique restaurant menus such as "On an Imaginary Planet," "Under the Ocean," "In a Dollhouse or Tiny Town," "Stuffed Animal Restaurant Menu"—or create your own themes.

CAVEMAN JOE'S DELUXE RESTAURANT
MENU ALA PREHISTORIC

SPECIAL	*	*
COMPLETE DINNER—$2.08	*SPECIAL CHILDRENS PORTION*	
STEGASAURUS SOUP	HALF PRICE LITTLER PORTION	
SHREDDED BIRD BRAIN SALAD	NO SOUP ONLY SALAD	
BREADED BONES	STONE BOX GIVEN FREE TO KEEP	
SNAKE PUDDING	UNFINISHED FOOD IN	

ALA CARTE

SHREDDED BRONTASAURUS BONES———————————— $2.98

SNAKE STEAK (MUSHROOMS—5¢ EXTRA———————————— $5.82 1/2

ROAST DUCKBILL DINOSAUR DELUXE SUPER———————————— $10.02

TOASTED TEETH WITH BLUE BLOOD TOPPING———————————— $4.24 1/4

BUTTER BASTED BEEK COVERED WITH SNAKE SKIN———————————— $260.39

EYEBALL ROASTED OR FRIED———————————— $.96 1/2

DESSERTS

BLUBBER PUDDING———————————— $.19

GRATED HORN PIES (ALA MUD)———————————— $.25—ALA MUD 5¢ MORE

SLICED TAIL PIE WITH ICE AGE CREAM———————————— $.91 1/2

TAR PIT PUDDING———————————— $2.00

ICED BLOOD OF DINOSAUR———————————— $.27 A GLASS

NOSTRIL OF DINOSAUR MILKSHAKE———————————— $.11

MUSHEY MALT———————————— $300.59 (VERY RARE MUSH)

LAVA SODA———————————— $3.24 (FRESH FROM VOLCANO

WE HOPE YOU ENJOYED YOUR MEAL   *COME AGAIN SOON!*

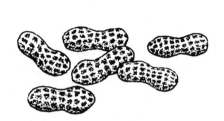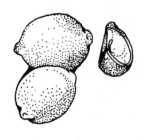

Science Experiments for Older Children

Kids can learn a lot about science by experimenting with food, and a lot about food by learning the science of it. Older children love to make bubbling concoctions and peer into microscopes. Some of the scientific concepts that can be experienced while doing food experiments are:

- ❑ solutions and crystals (sugar, salt)
- ❑ the properties of acids and bases (baking soda, vinegar)
- ❑ emulsification (mayonnaise)
- ❑ the properties of starches and sugars (caramelized sugar, tapioca)
- ❑ denaturing of proteins (sour milk, scrambled eggs)
- ❑ oxidation (apples treated with lemon juice)
- ❑ the life cycles of organisms like yeasts, molds, and bacteria (yogurt, bread)
- ❑ the action of enzymes (meat tenderizer)

Interested in learning more? (We must confess to a fascination with science experiments ourselves. Some things you never outgrow!) There are some very good books available that can show you how to set kids up in their own "laboratories."

Science Experiments You Can Eat. Vicki Cobb. New York: Harper & Row, Publishers, 1972.

Foodworks: Over 100 Science Activities and Fascinating Facts That Explore the Magic of Food. Ontario Science Centre. Massachusetts: Addison-Wesley Publishing Company, Inc., 1987.

Science Fun with Peanuts and Popcorn. Rose Wyler. New York: Julian Mesner, 1986.

APPENDIX A

References

Chapter One—A Basic Scheme for Nutrition Education

1. *Choose Well, Be Well: A Curriculum Guide for Preschool and Kindergarten.* California State Department of Education, 1982.

Chapter Two—The Social Aspects of Food

Barnett, Kathy: Hunger: In *Discovering the World: Empowering Children to Value Themselves, Others and the Earth.* Philadelphia, PA: New Society Publishers, 1990.

Bjork, Christina and Anderson, Lena. *Linnea's Windowsill Garden.* Translated by Joan Sandin, Stockholm: R & S. Books, 1988.

Derman-Sparks, Louise and the A.B.C. Task Force. *Anti-Bias Curriculum: Tools for Empowering Young Children.* Washington, D.C.: National Association for the Education of Young Children, 1989.

Earthworks Group. *50 Simple Things Kids Can Do to Save the Earth.* Kansas City: Andrews and McMeel, 1990.

Elkington, J., Hailes, J., Hill, D. & Makower, J. *Going Green: A Kid's Handbook to Saving the Planet.* New York: The Penguin Group, 1990.

Hadingham, Evan & Janet. *Garbage! Where It Comes From, Where It Goes.* New York: Simon and Schuster, Inc., 1990.

Hopkins, Susan: Families. In *Discovering the World: Empowering Children to Value Themselves, Others and the Earth.*

Olmstead, Kathy: World Foods. In *Discovering the World: Empowering Children to Value Themselves, Others and the Earth.*

Rubin, Laurie. *Food First Curriculum: An Integrated Curriculum for Grade 6.* San Francisco, CA: Institute for Food and Development Policy, 1984.

Schwab, Michael G.: Participatory Research with Children: A New Approach to Nutrition Education. In *Journal of Nutrition Education* 21: 184B, 1989.

U.S. Department of Agriculture, Human Nutrition Information Service. *Shopping for Food and Making Meals in Minutes Using the Dietary Guidelines.* Washington, D.C.: U.S. Government Printing Office, 1989.

Chapter Three—Activities for Kids

1. Hertzler, A.: Preschoolers' food handling skills—motor development. *Journal of Nutrition Education* 21: 100B, 1989.

APPENDIX B

Resources

Publications

General Nutrition

Nutrition Action Healthletter
Center for Science in the Public Interest
Suite 300, 1875 Connecticut Avenue, N.W.
Washington, D.C. 20009-5728
$14.95/year
Reports on the latest nutrition research and consumer issues; includes great recipes.

University of California, Berkeley Wellness Letter
Wellness Letter Subscription Department
P.O. Box 420148
Palm Coast, Florida 32142
$20/year
"The newsletter of nutrition, fitness, and stress management"

Tufts University
Diet & Nutrition Letter
P.O. Box 57857
Boulder, CO 80322-7857
1-800-274-7581
Subscription $20 per year (12 issues)

Consumer Information Catalog Booklets (When ordering free booklets, you must enclose $1.00 to help defray costs.) To order sales and free booklets, include check or money order payable to: Superintendent of Documents, and mail to:
R. Woods
Consumer Information Center-T
P.O. Box 100
Pueblo, Colorado 81002

Dietary Guidelines Booklets. Four colorful magazine-style booklets to help put the USDA/HHS Dietary Guidelines for Americans into everyday practice:

1. *"Eating Better When Eating Out"* How to compare calories and nutrients; with sample menu to help build food selection skills. 19 pp. (1989. USDA/HHS); Item # 123W. $1.50.

2. *"Making Bag Lunches, Snacks, and Desserts."* Ideas for creative hot and cold lunches; snack and dessert ideas with less fat and sugar. 31 pp. (1989. USDA/HHS); Item # 124W. $2.50.

3. *"Preparing Foods and Planning Menus."* Sample daily menus at two different calorie levels with recipes and tips for cutting down fat, sugars and sodium. 31 pp. (1989. USDA/HHS); Item # 125W. $2.50.

4. *"Shopping for Food and Making Meals in Minutes."* An aisle-by-aisle shopping guide to the supermarket; includes time saving recipes. 35 pp. (1989. USDA/HHS); Item #126W. $3.00.

Other booklets from Consumer Information Catalog:

"Eating for Life." How food choices can reduce your risk of developing cancer and heart diseases. Tips on buying and preparing food and eating out. 23 pp. (1988. NIH); Item #118W. $1.00.

"Nutritive Value of Foods." Listings for over 900 foods—calories, sodium, cholesterol and more. 72 pp. (1988. USDA); 120W. $2.75.

"Planning a Diet for a Healthy Heart." Learn how to reduce the risk of heart disease by cutting down on fat and cholesterol. 6 pp. (1989. FDA); Item #525W. Free.

"Food Additives." Explains why chemicals are added to foods and how this is regulated. 4 pp. (1987. FDA); Item #523W. Free.

Food News for Consumers. Up-to-date articles on food safety, health and nutrition, food concerns. Annual subscription/4 issues (USDA); Item #251W. $5.00.

Jane Brody's Nutrition Book by Jane Brody Toronto: Bantam Books, 1987

The New Laurel's Kitchen by, L. Robertson, C. Flinders, and, B. Ruppenthal. Berkeley: Ten Speed Press, 1986.

Child Nutrition

Child of Mine: Feeding With Love and Good Sense by Ellyn Satter, RD, MS, MSSW. Palo Alto: Bull Publishing Co.,1986.

How to Get Your Kid to Eat . . . But Not Too Much by Ellyn Satter RD, MS, MSSW. Palo Alto: Bull Publishing Co., 1987.

The Relationship Between Nutrition and Learning: A School Employees' Guide to Information and Action. National Education Association
Human and Civil Rights
1201 Sixteenth Street, N.W.
Washington, D.C., 20036
(800) 229-4200
Describes the importance of nutrition for optimum learning and what schools can do to ensure that all children have access to good nutrition.

Allergies

Allergy Products Directory
Prologue Publications
P.O. Box 640
Menlo Park, CA 94026.
Listings for food products and their sources.

"Tasty Rice Recipes for Those With Allergies"
Rice Council of America
P.O. Box 74021
Houston, TX 77274

"Gluten-Free Diet"
National Celiac-Sprue Society
5 Jeffrey Road
Wayland, MA 01778

"Delicious Milk-Free Recipes"
Loma Linda Foods
11503 Pierce Street
Riverside, CA 92515

Coping With Food Allergy by Claude A. Frazier, M.D. Revised Edition. New York: Times Books, 1985.
Good information on food allergies with extensive recipe section.

Caring and Cooking for the Allergic Child by Linda Thomas. New York: Sterling Publishing, 1980.

Diabetes

American Diabetes Association, Inc.
Diabetes Information Service Center
1660 Duke Street
Alexandria, VA 22314
(800)ADA-DISC
Also local affiliates.

Diabetes Mellitus—A Practical Handbook by Sue K. Milchovich, RN, BSN, CDE, and Barbara Dunn-Long, RD. Palo Alto: Bull Publishing Co., 1990.

Exchanges for All Occasions: Meeting the Challenge of Diabetes by Marion J. Franz, RD, MS. Minnesota: Diabetes Center, Inc., 1987. Diabetic exchange lists, recipes, and hints for managing events like illness, travel and children's parties.

Kids, Food, and Diabetes by Gloria Loring Chicago: Contemporary Books, Inc., 1986. Written by an actress and mother of a child with diabetes, this book is full of guidelines, recipes, and "coping hints" for dealing with diabetes.

Special Needs

"Feeding Young Children with Cleft Lip and Palate" (booklet, $1.50)
Minnesota Dietetic Association
1821 U. Avenue, Suite S-280
St. Paul, MN 55104

United Cerebral Palsy Associations, Inc.
66 East 34th Street
New York, NY 10016
(212) 481-6344

American Occupational Therapy Assoc., Inc.
1383 Piccard Drive
P.O. Box 1725
Rockville, MD 20850-4375

Mealtimes for Persons with Severe Handicaps by R. Perske, A. Clifton, B.M. McLean and J. Ishler Stein. Baltimore: Paul H. Brookes, 1986.
Managing the School-Age Child With a Chronic Health Condition, Georgianna Larson, RN, PNP, MPH, Editor.
Minnesota: DCI Publishing, 1988.

Food Safety

For Our Kids' Sake: How to Protect Your Child Against Pesticides in Food by Anne Witte Garland. San Francisco: Sierra Club Books, 1989.

FDA Consumer.
Annual subscription (10 issues), $12.00 Item #252W Articles on safety of food, drugs, and cosmetics and their regulation by the Food and Drug Administration.

Food News for Consumers
Annual subscription (4 issues), $5.00 Item #251W.

To subscribe to *FDA Consumer* or *Food News for Consumers* make check or money order payable to Superintendent of Documents and send order to:
Consumer Information Center - T
P.O. Box 100
Pueblo, CO 81002

Cookbooks

Jane Brody's Good Food Book by Jane Brody. Toronto: Bantam Books, 1987.
More than 350 healthful recipes and lots of good basic nutrition information.

The New Laurel's Kitchen by L. Robertson, C. Flinders, and B. Ruppenthal.
Berkeley: Ten Speed Press, 1986.

Healthwise Quantity Cookbook by S.Turner, MPH, RD and V. Aronowitz, MPH, RD. Washington, D.C.: Center for Science in the Public Interest, 1990.

Cooking Light magazine.
P.O. Box 830549
Birmingham, AL 35282-9810

Microwave Diet Cookery by M. Cone & T. Snyder. New York: Simon and Schuster, 1988. How to use the microwave oven to prepare low-calorie, healthy meals.

Kitchen Lore

Keeping Food Fresh: How to Choose and Store Everything You Eat, by Janet Bailey. Revised Edition. New York: Harper & Row, Publishers. New York, 1989.This book contains fascinating information on selecting and storing foods and general tips for food safety.

Kitchen Science: A Guide to Knowing the How's and Why's for Fun and Success in the Kitchen. Revised Edition. Boston: Houghton Mifflin Company, 1989. For those who wonder— How do nonstick coatings work? Why does meat get tougher as it cooks? Why does red cabbage turn bluish purple when cooked?

Social and Environmental Concerns

Discovering the World: Empowering Children to Value Themselves, Others and the Earth. S. Hopkins and J. Winters, ed. Philadelphia, PA: New Society Publishers, 1990.

Anti-Bias Curriculum: Tools for Empowering Young Children by Louise Derman-Sparks and the A.B.C. Task Force. Washington, D.C.: National Association for the Education of Young Children, 1989. (companion video also available)

Food First Curriculum: An integrated curriculum for Grade 6 by Laurie Rubin. San Francisco, CA: Institute for Food and Development Policy, 1984.

Teaching and Learning in a Diverse World: Multicultural Education for Young Children by Patricia G. Ramsey. Available from Toys 'n Things Press; (800) 423-8309.

An Introductory Guide to Bilingual Bicultural/ Multicultural Education: Beyond Tacos, Eggrolls and Grits by Gloria Gomez. Dubuque: Kendall/Hunt Publishing Company, 1982.

Skipping Stones
Aprovecho Institute
80574 Hazelton Rd.
Cottage Grove, OR 97424; (503) 942-9434.
$15/year (quarterly).
A multi-ethnic international children's magazine.

50 Simple Things Kids Can Do to Save the Earth by The Earthworks Group. Kansas City: Andrews and McMeel, 1990.

Children's Book Press
1461 Ninth Avenue
San Francisco, CA 94122
(415) 664-8500
A non-profit children's book publisher, specializing in multicultural children's literature.

Mothers and Others for a Livable Planet.
Natural Resources Defense Council
40 West 20th Street.
New York, NY 10011
(212) 727-2700
A special project dedicated to environmental problems that especially affect children. *TLC*, its newsletter, has a pull-out section for children.

Kids for Saving Earth
P.O. Box 47247
Plymouth, MN 55447-0247
(612) 525-0002
International membership organization for kids who pledge to "be a defender of my planet." Members receive certificate, resources, guidebook and more.

Garbage! Where It Comes From, Where It Goes by Evan & Janet Hadingham. New York: Simon and Schuster, Inc., 1990.

Going Green: A Kid's Handbook to Saving the Planet by J.Elkington, J. Hailes, D. Hill, and J. Makower. New York: Puffin Books, 1990.

Shopping for a Better World: The Quick and Easy Guide to Socially Responsible Supermarket Shopping
Council on Economic Priorities
30 Irving Place
New York, NY 10003-9990
(800) 822-6435
Provides the information necessary for consumers to select products made by companies whose policies and practices they support.

The Consumer Guide to Home Energy Savings
American Council for an Energy Efficient Economy
1001 Connecticut Avenue, NW, #535
Washington, DC 20036
(202) 429-8873
$6.95

Garbage: The Practical Journal for the Environment
P.O. Box 51647
Boulder, CO 80321-1647
An excellent resource for home waste-reduction.

Nutrition Activities with Kids

Creative Food Experiences for Children by Mary T. Goodwin and G. Pollen. Revised Edition. Washington, D.C.: Center for Science in the Public Interest, 1980. A classic guide to teaching children aged 3 to 10 about good nutrition.

Eat, Think, and Be Healthy! by Paula K. Zeller and M. Jacobsen, Ph.D. Washington, D.C.: Center for Science in the Public Interest, 1987. Nutrition activities for kids grade 3-6. Includes recipes for foods kids can make. Handouts. Basic nutrition, smart consumerism.

I Love Animals and Broccoli by Debra Wasserman and Charles Stahler. Baltimore: 1985.
The Vegetarian Resource Group
P.O. Box 1463, Baltimore MD 21203. $5.00.
Healthy eating, caring about animals, world hunger.

Cooking With Kids

Cook and Learn: Pictorial Single Portion Recipes by Beverly Veitch and Thelma Harms. Menlo Park: Addison-Wesley Publishing Company, 1981.

Kid's Cooking: A Very Slightly Messy Manual by the Editors of Klutz Press. Palo Alto: Klutz Press, 1987.

"Easy Menu Ethnic Cookbooks."
> *Cooking the African Way*
> *Cooking the Caribbean Way*
> *Cooking the Chinese Way*
> *Cooking the English Way*
> *Cooking the French Way*
> *Cooking the German Way*
> *Cooking the Greek Way*
> *Cooking the Hungarian Way*
> *Cooking the Indian Way*
> *Cooking the Israeli Way*
> *Cooking the Italian Way*
> *Cooking the Japanese Way*
> *Cooking the Korean Way*
> *Cooking the Lebanese Way*
> *Cooking the Mexican Way*
> *Cooking the Norwegian Way*
> *Cooking the Polish Way*
> *Cooking the Russian Way*
> *Cooking the Spanish Way*
> *Cooking the Thai Way*
> *Cooking the Vietnamese Way*
> —Lerner Publications
>   Company, Minneapolis

Miscellaneous Books

NAEYC Early Childhood Resources Catalog
1834 Connecticut Avenue, N.W.
Washington, D.C., 20009-5786
(800) 424-2460
Outstanding books, pamphlets, posters, etc., for early childhood educators from the National Association for the Education of Young Children.

Toys 'n Things Press: Resources for the Early Childhood Professional
A division of Resources for Child Caring
450 North Syndicate, Suite 5
St. Paul, MN 55104
(800) 423-8309
Excellent books and other learning materials for adults and children.

Sisters' Choice Recordings and Books
1450 Sixth Street
Berkeley, CA 94710
(415) 524-5804
Books and tapes about environmentalism, multicultural issues, animal rights, and other social concerns.

Supplies

Earth-Friendly Products

Seventh Generation, Products for a Healthy
Planet
Colchester, VT 05446-1672
(800) 441-2538
Energy-saving devices, ecological household
cleaners, recycling supplies. Catalog includes
lots of tips.

Co-op America Catalog
2100 M Street, Suite 403
Washington, DC 20063
(202) 223-1881
Ecological products, energy-saving devices,
etc.

Ecco Bella, The Environmental Store
6 Provost Square, Suite 602
Caldwell, NJ 07006
(800) 888-5320
Non-animal tested, bio-degradable products.

EcoSource, Products for a Safer, Cleaner
World
9051 Mill Station Rd.
Sebastopol, CA 95472
(800) 688-8345

Gardener's Supply
128 Intervale Road
Burlington, VT 05401
(802) 863-1700
Chemical-free pest control supplies,
composting equipment, etc.

Specialty Foods

Ener-G-Foods, Inc.
5960 - 1st Avenue S.
P.O. Box 84487
Seattle, WA 98124-5787
(800) 331-5222
Food products for gluten-free, wheat-free,
milk-free, soy-free, and corn-free diets.
Recipes also available.

Fearn Natural Foods
4520 James Place
Melrose Park, IL 60160
Baking mixes for allergy diets; found in most
health-food stores.

Loma Linda Foods
11503 Pierce Street
Riverside, CA 92515
A variety of food products for allergy diets.

Learning Materials and Toys

Good Food Puppets. Seven colorful
puppets—Milk, Chicken, Fish, Apple, Carrot,
Bread, SuperBean: $49.98/set. Good Food
Puppets Puppetry Book with scripts, lessons,
songs, etc.: $12.98/book. Complete set:
$59.98. To order, add 15% postage and
handling fee.
Yummy Designs, P.O. Box 1851-D, Walla
Walla, WA 99362; (509)525-2072

Lingo, bingo-type game which familiarizes
children with foods around the world in
three languages (for 3–10 year olds).
UNICEF
1 Children's Boulevard, P.O. 182233
Chattanooga, TN 37422
(800) For-Kids

HearthSong
P.O. Box B
Sebastopol, CA 95473-0601
(800) 325-2502
Catalog of wonderful toys, crafts, books,
games, etc.

Animal Town
P.O. Box 485
Healdsburg, CA 95448
(800) 445-8642
Catalog of nature games and books,
cooperative games, posters, toys and much
more. Beautiful!

Music for Little People
P.O. Box 1460, 1144 Redway Drive
Redway CA 95560
(800) 346-4445
Children's audio and video tapes, musical
instruments. Materials which emphasize
multi-cultural, social and environmental
awareness.

Lakeshore® Learning Materials.
2695 E. Dominguez Street. P.O. Box 6261
Carson, CA 90749
(800) 421-5354
Play foods (includes foods from various cultures), kitchen equipment, child-sized furniture; supplies for classroom cooking projects, etc.

Fisher-Price®
East Aurora, New York 14052
Super Mart Super Cart shopping cart comes with play money and groceries; Magic Scan Checkout Counter and other Fun with Food™ toys.

Miscellaneous

Fat Finder®.. $5.45/$7.45 with 60-page book.
Vitaerobics
41-905 Boardwalk, Suite B
Palm Desert, CA 92260-5141
41/2-inch diameter wheel for quickly and accurately determining percentage of fat calories in foods. (16-inch demonstration model also available.)

Lead Alert Kit $29.95 + $3.50 shipping
Francon Enterprises, Inc.
P.O. Box 300321, Seattle, WA 98103
(800) 359-9000.
Tests pottery, toys, metalware, and decorated glassware for leaching of lead.

Table Manners for Everyday Use by handy vision. A humorous instructional video that can be enjoyed by both children and adults. Available from Sybervision Systems, Inc.
(800) 678-0887.

National Dairy Council®,
Order Department*
6300 North River Road
Rosemont, IL 60018-4233
(708) 696-1860, Ext. 220
Curriculum packages for children, preschool through high school, and other consumer materials; some available in Spanish.
*Or check your telephone directory for a local Dairy Council® affiliate near you.

American Heart Association
44 East 23rd Street
New York, NY 10010
Check your telephone directory for a local AHA affiliate. A variety of educational materials are available, including schoolsite health promotion curricula.

The Vegetarian Resource Group
P.O. Box 1463
Baltimore, MD 21203
(301) 366-VEGE
Many free or low-cost teaching materials about vegetarianism, suitable for preschoolers through teens. Send for a resource list.

Community Resources and Organizations

Who to Ask for General Information

Local agencies:

- City, county, or state health department
- Cooperative Extension Service
- Women, Infants, and Children (WIC) supplemental food program
- Universities with programs in nutrition, dietetics, or food service management
- Child Care Food Program
- Affiliates of the American Heart Association, American Diabetes Association, American Cancer Society, or Dairy Council®

Consumer Information/Baby Food:

- Beech-Nut   (800) 523-6633
- Earth's Best   (800) 442-422
- Gerber   (800) 443-7237
- Heinz   (800) USA-BABY
- Simply Pure   (800) 426-7873

Food Safety Questions

Food and Drug Administration
Office of Consumer Affairs HFE-88
5600 Fishers Lane
Rockville, MD 20857
(301) 443-3170

USDA Meat and Poultry Hotline
USDA-FSIS, Room 1165-S
Washington, D.C. 20250
(800) 535-4555
(10 a.m. – 4 p.m. weekdays)

EPA Safe Drinking Water Hotline
(800) 426-4791
(202) 382-5533 in Washington, D.C.

Help for Children with Handicapping Conditions

- nutritionists in state and local health departments
- pediatric nutritionists, occupational therapists, and physical therapists in programs serving children with special needs, e.g., genetics treatment centers, diagnostic evaluation centers, and hospitals affiliated with a medical school

How to Get the Most Information From a Product Label

The nutrition label on a food product should help you decide whether it would be a good choice for a healthful diet. Unfortunately, food labels as they are now used cause a lot of confusion. As this book goes to press, new regulations are being formulated that should make food labels more helpful. In the meantime, here's some information that will help you separate fact from fantasy when you're reading the information on a box of cereal or can of juice!

❑ Nutrition labeling is not *required* on all packaged foods. Foods must be labeled if they have been fortified with vitamins, minerals, or protein, or if a claim is being made regarding the nutrient content of the product. Some manufacturers label their food products voluntarily.

❑ A nutrition label must list the calorie, protein, carbohydrate, fat, sodium, iron, vitamins A and C, calcium, thiamin, riboflavin, and niacin content of the product. Remember, though, that these aren't the only nutrients you need.

❑ Check the serving size carefully. Sometimes unreasonably small or large serving sizes are listed in order to make the product seem more nutritionally desirable (low in calories, for example).

❑ Most foods at least have ingredient lists on their labels. The ingredients are listed in order by weight, from the most to the least. For example, if butter is the first ingredient on the list, there is more butter in the product than any other ingredient.

❑ You will need to know alternative names for certain food components in order to really get a clear picture of how much of them a product contains.

Sugar:
brown sugar	dextrose
honey	fructose
corn syrup	sucrose
corn syrup solids	maltose
invert sugar	molasses
maple syrup	

Sodium:
salt	monosodium glutamate
baking soda	sodium benzoate
sodium caseinate	sodium nitrate
sodium nitrite	sodium phosphate
sodium propionate	

❑ The fat content of a food is listed in grams. But what you're probably interested in is "what's the amount of fat here relative to the calories?" There are two ways you can find this out. One is to perform some quick math: Each gram of fat has 9 calories. Multiply the grams of fat in a serving by 9 to get the calories contributed from fat. Divide this product by the total number of calories and multiply by 100. Voila! You've calculated the percentage of calories from fat. Alternatively, you can use a handy little gadget called a "Fat Finder" that does the math for you.

Fat Finder®
$5.45 from Vitaerobics
41-905 Boardwalk, Suite B
Palm Desert, CA 92260-5141
(800) 323-8042

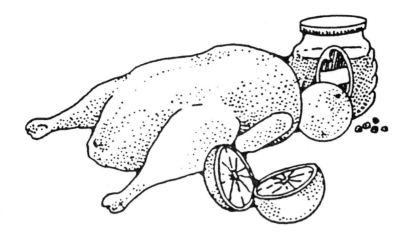

❏ Don't be misled by percentage signs. A food that's labeled "95% fatfree" does not get just 5% of its calories from fat. It contains 5% fat by weight, and the heaviest component of many foods is water. Since fat has a lot of calories, the food could still be relatively high in fat.

❏ Know what the various terms on labels really mean:

- sodium-free = less than 5 mg sodium/serving
- very low sodium = 35 mg or less sodium/serving
- low sodium = 140 mg or less sodium/serving
- reduced sodium = at least a 75% reduction in sodium compared with the usual product
- unsalted, no salt added = no salt added during processing of a food usually made with salt
- cholesterol-free = 2 mg or less cholesterol/serving
- low cholesterol = 20 mg or less cholesterol/serving
- reduced cholesterol = 75% or more reduction in cholesterol from the usual product
- extra lean = meat or poultry contains no more than 5% fat by weight
- lean, lowfat = meat or poultry contains no more than 10% fat by weight
- light, leaner = meat or poultry that has a 25% or more reduction in fat from the usual product

Think of Mother Earth When You're Shopping

Most of us have grown up during the "disposables" or "throw-away" generations. Now that we are faced with the dire consequences, we find ourselves struggling to change some very ingrained environmentally harmful habits. With less than 5% of the world's population, our nation generates 25% of its pollutants and more than 30% of its garbage.[6] Did you know that every day Americans throw out an average of 4 pounds of garbage each. That totals a daily garbage heap of 438,000 tons—enough to fill 63,000 garbage trucks![7] By becoming "green" consumers we can directly reduce the amount of waste.

Here's how to shop with ecology in mind:

- ❏ First and foremost—if you don't really need it, don't buy it!
- ❏ Choose reusable items over disposable items whenever possible.
- ❏ Be picky about packaging . . .
    - look for products that have minimal packaging
    - choose products packaged in recycled (look for the symbol) or recyclable materials, or in reusable containers
    - choose products packaged in materials that are most easily recyclable in your community
    - buy eggs in cardboard cartons rather than foam plastic

- avoid purchasing anything in foam plastic
- let the store manager know why you are making these choices
- write or call the manufacturers and let them know why you've chosen to buy or not to buy their products (You can usually find their address and phone number on the container. Many companies list an 800 phone number for consumers.)

❏ Bring your own canvas or string bags with you when you shop.

❏ When you must use bags from the store, choose paper which can be recycled over plastic (most of which are neither biodegradable or recyclable). Reuse bags by bringing them the next time you shop.

❏ Read labels—try not to purchase products with harmful ingredients.

❏ Buy the large size or buy in bulk.

❏ When you do make purchases in recyclable containers, be sure to actually recycle them.

❏ Talk to your children about why you are making these choices; this will help them develop their own "ecology awareness."

Basic Guide to Measurements

Reminder: Help with measuring is a great way to enable children to participate in the cooking process. In fact, checking the accuracy of your measuring equipment can make an interesting math and science activity.

Standard U.S. Liquid Measurements

3 teaspoons	=	1 tablespoon
4 tablespoons	=	1/4 cup or 2 ounces
5 1/3 tablespoons	=	1/3 cup or 2 2/3 ounces
12 tablespoons	=	3/4 cup or 6 ounces
16 tablespoons	=	1 cup or 8 ounces
2 cups	=	1 pint
2 pints	=	1 liquid quart
4 quarts	=	1 liquid gallon

❑

Canned Goods Weights & Measures

8 ounces	=	1 cup
10 1/2–12 ounces	=	1 1/4 cups
14–16 ounces	=	1 1/2 cups
16–17 ounces	=	2 cups
1 lb. 4 ounces	=	2 1/2 cups
1 lb. 13 ounces	=	3 1/2 cups

Index